The Wonderful Adventure of Loving Ourselves

A Journey in Healing, Forgiveness and Love

By Robert Kauffman

The Wonderful Adventure of Loving Ourselves:
A Journey in Healing, Forgiveness and Love

By Robert Kauffman

Published by Legacy Press Books
A subsidiary of S & P Productions, Inc.
311 Main Street, Suite D
El Segundo, CA 90245
310-640-8885
www.legacypressbooks.com

Published and Printed in the United States of America

ISBN: 978-1-950326-17-4

The content contained in The Wonderful Adventure of Loving Ourselves: A Journey in Healing, Forgiveness and Love is for informational purposes only. The content is not intended to be a substitute for medical or psychological advice, diagnosis or treatment. Always seek the advice of your physician or other qualified healthcare provider with any questions you may have regarding a medical or mental health condition. Always seek the advice of qualified professionals in matters relating to any business undertakings.

DEDICATION

So many people have helped me grow and learn, and I'm grateful for all of them.

I want to acknowledge my editor, Lynn Sanders, for recognizing the value of my memoir, and her creative editing in bringing this story to life.

I'm proud and inspired by my daughter, Katie, and son, Tim, who have become far better parents to my grandchildren than I was ever for them.

And I'm deeply inspired by my wife, Kit, who not only opens many spiritual doors for me, but also accompanies me through them.

Endorsement for *The Wonderful Adventure of Loving Ourselves; A Journey in Healing, Forgiveness, and Love.*:

Listen closely to the authentic voice of Bob Kauffman as he talks to you in *The Wonderful Adventure of Loving Ourselves; A Journey in Healing, Forgiveness, and Love.* I should know, because I first met Bob as his field student at G D Searle in 1978. He was head of the employee assistance program there. As I met key executives in the firm, almost every one talked about Bob in glowing terms. The stories of how he had helped them and their families blew me away. One particularly tough executive said Bob saved his life and kept him from killing himself.

Most important, however, is what he taught me that he is teaching you in this book—to be more loving to yourself. I first met Bob in the second year of my MSW studies. I had gone into my studies deeply trained in humanistic psychology approaches from Transactional Analysis to Gestalt and I was also being trained in Contemporary Adlerian therapy. I was cocky and was consistently shot down by professors and senior staff in my first year field placement, deservedly in many instances. I was a scared shrunken student when I began working under Bob. I was like an abused animal. Any therapy I delivered was simply more ways to criticize myself and find out what was wrong with me. My first year supervision never said anything other than criticisms after listening to recordings of my sessions. As my second year supervisor, I would review sessions with Bob. I reviewed each session, telling him everything I think I did wrong or could have improved. His response was a life turning moment for me. I am a child of a mother whose mothering philosophy had no room for understanding or kind words. Bob was so different. He would invariably say something like, "Bob, each time we talk, you tell me what you could have done better, and I am consistently struck by how effective you are." This quote was only the first of several significant life altering interactions I was to have with Bob over the years.

~ Dr. Bob Wright

Former student, partner, and award-winning bestselling author, educator, and researcher in human potential and lifelong learning.

TABLE OF CONTENTS

WHAT CRITICAL THINKING SKILLS
DO WE NEED?

There is a Biblical saying, "Love thy neighbor as yourself." Well, if most people were going to love me the way they love themselves, I wouldn't want to be anywhere around them because they don't love themselves. They don't realize that commandment is really two commandments.

The first is to fully love yourself. The second is to fully love others. If you learn to do the first, the second one will be easy. As you will see, you are connected to everyone around you, and they are incredible souls just like you.

I experienced many losses in my life which were very painful. I have learned a lot about myself and life from going through those losses. I want to share my discoveries to help you. I feel my purpose in life is to teach others to fully love themselves. It challenges me every day. It's not always an easy task.

Being a 78-year-old man who still does what he loves, I've had plenty of time to reflect on my life. Looking back, I can now see how my life lessons could provide insights to others on their life paths.

My philosophy is, "The body is like a box of tools. It's not the carpenter. We are the carpenters. We chose to come into this body to become more loving… to love ourselves and love others. This world is a school, and it's for us to learn to love more fully." I've found if people love themselves fully, they will automatically love others.

Critical Skill #1: **To fully love ourselves, we need to know ourselves and who *we* really are**.

When this happens, we realize who others are and that leads us to love them. We realize they are incredible souls like ourselves, and we are profoundly connected.

I believe we are wonderful, creative souls who choose to take on a body in this physical world. We're here to learn what love truly is. We're on a path to become more mature as souls, and ultimately become co-workers with God.

From my perspective, every day I get to sit down with creators (my clients) and coach wonderful creators, who are a little confused about who they really are. I have the privilege of believing in my clients until they begin to believe in themselves.

Critical Skill #2: **Create new beliefs that serve you.**

All my clients come in with stories about their lives, the beliefs they created about themselves and the world. They're busy blaming themselves and others for their plights, and not feeling good about themselves. They often feel trapped, stuck and afraid of change.

Does this sound familiar? My clients don't see how they create the lives they're living. Instead, they typically feel like victims of the world or life. People come in to see me for many reasons and types of problems. Many are experiencing a great deal of upset, anxiety, panic, PTSD, depression, and pain. Others come in to learn how to enhance their lives and be more creative.

My work is to help my clients recognize the beliefs that are controlling them and making them unhappy. These beliefs imprison my clients and keep them living unhappy, unfulfilling lives. My work helps clients create new beliefs that serve them and help them grow, so they can live joyfully.

Critical Skill #3: What to do to change your life direction.

My job is to help people understand not only how they create their lives, but if they don't like its direction, what they need to do to change it. I use many therapies of healing to serve them, and ultimately, it makes their lives more fulfilling.

Whether I'm with individuals, couples, families, businesses, veterans or athletes, I've found that people need help in ultimately loving themselves.

To serve as many people as possible, I decided to reveal what I uncovered through my journey in life. Many of my discoveries came with heart-breaking pain and anguish. It's not necessary to suffer so much pain in order to learn what I learned. I just did it the hard way. I don't recommend that kind of experience.

Since I don't want you to go through the pain I endured, my goal is to help each one of you learn what I learned. This book can provide a shortcut into the joy of loving yourself, without having to deal with the suffering. Two basic things you'll need are, a clear pathway to follow in creating what you want, and solid support to follow your vision.

Critical Skill #4:   How to love yourself.

Ultimately, if you love yourself and learn how to take care of yourself, you'll better enjoy your life. Makes sense, right?

Along the way, you'll find what a great creator you are. You'll discover how to create a rich and fulfilling life. And you'll make a difference in other lives too.

Appreciating yourself is often a difficult task for many. Let's try to make it easier and more fun!

Let's begin!

CHAPTER 1
Tracing The Roots

By sharing the roots of my story, I hope you'll gain a deeper understanding of yourself. Our emotional history can be traced back over generations. I invite you to investigate your own family's roots. Get in touch with older relatives. We inherit both genetic and emotional patterns.

What emotional blockages did your families face?

How has this affected you?

Once you learn about your family's emotional history, you'll be able to better understand your own emotional baggage.

Let me share the roots behind my own story. My beginning was in a little town, Bremen, Indiana, on a 100-acre vegetable farm. As the third of six children, who all arrived in 8 1/2 years, my parents oversaw a busy household. There were two homes on our farm. One belonged to Uncle Roy and Aunt Fern, and the other belonged to our family. You can be certain that everyone participated in doing chores!

Life Lesson #1:   It's important to learn responsibility at an early age.

The Kauffman family arrived in the colonies from Berne,

Switzerland to escape persecution for their beliefs. They were primarily farmers and shopkeepers, moving west to Ohio, Indiana, Illinois, Wisconsin, Iowa and south to Virginia. A Kauffman woman married a Lincoln man. She became grandmother or great grandmother to Abraham Lincoln. Yes, Abraham Lincoln is my distant cousin. Perhaps it's in our genes, but we both shared personal heartaches on our road to fulfillment.

My dad's side of the family repressed their feelings. Everyone was very stoic. My great-grandfather fought in the Civil War as an artillery man on the Union side and returned home from the war practically deaf. He was not a very happy man. I believe he suffered from Post Traumatic Stress Disorder (PTSD), which affected my grandfather and father.

No one seemed close to each other. Grandfather died before any of us were born, and I heard he didn't like religion. He forbade my grandmother and dad to go to church. Interestingly, the Sunday after my grandfather died, guess where my grandmother went? To church!

Life Lesson #2: We inherit emotional patterns from our family.

When the depression hit, my dad was graduating from high school. Although he wanted to go to college, he didn't have the money to attend. For three years, dad worked to save up enough money to go to college. Then, he attended a work-study college, Blackburn College in Carlinville, Illinois.

At Blackburn College, my dad met my mother, who came from a strong Catholic upbringing. Although my mom's father died before I was born, I heard he was a genuinely nice, gentle man. He sorted mail on the railroad car between St. Louis and Chicago. When the train came through Carlinville, my grandmother took food to the train for him.

Grandfather died on Christmas Day when my grandmother was in her late fifties. She never celebrated Christmas after that. Keeping her sadness inside, she'd give us our Christmas present on Thanksgiving.

Life Lesson #3: Repressed emotions affect us.

As the second youngest of ten children, my mother's mother had a great deal of influence on me. In her small town, she was called "Aunt Susie" by everyone, often playing cards and having an occasional beer.

I remember being five or six, standing in our yard in Indiana, and hearing her tell me that this summer would probably be her last. That really scared me! I loved her so much.

How would I manage if she died? Somehow, she kept on living. I don't think my grandmother knew how what she said affected me. It wasn't until I was 37 years old that she passed away, and I was her pallbearer. She lived to be 97 years old.

My father's side of the family were shut down and depressed. My mom's side of the family worried and felt guilty.

REFLECTIONS

1. What mindset has been passed on to you that affects you now?

2. Can you identify emotional baggage from your family? What is it?

3. Why do you think the emotional patterns might have happened? (Hint: It helps to uncover your family's history.)

4. Do you feel it's possible to change your beliefs? (Hint: Yes!) Before you can change your beliefs, let's identify why you feel the way you do.

CHAPTER 2
Guilt Galloped In Our Family

A legacy of guilt certainly existed with my parents and got passed along to me. I never knew about my parents' very quick marriage until I was an adult. No one ever mentioned it. There was too much shame. Still, I was affected by this shadow of guilt as I was raised.

It started with a whirlwind romance. My mother was in her freshman year at Blackburn College when she met my father. He was a handsome sophomore. It was instant chemistry! They started dating and fell for each other. At some point, they must have thrown caution to the wind. People didn't talk about pre-marital sex in those days!

You can imagine their fear when suddenly, my mom missed her period. They both thought my mother was pregnant.

What a shock! What should they do? My mom was brought up as a Catholic, and my father wanted to do the right thing. Dad wasn't Catholic, but he wouldn't abandon her. They decided that the decent thing to do would be to get married.

Guilt, guilt, guilt…

It wasn't easy to find a priest that would marry them. What priest would marry them? Searching everywhere, they finally found a priest who married them in Plymouth, Indiana. It was done quickly and quietly. No one needed to know why they were getting married, right? They had known each other for less than a year.

But they were in for a second surprise. After the marriage, my parents found out that my mother wasn't pregnant after all! She had just missed her period.

Oh, the shame! The embarrassment! They both must have felt terribly guilty around the fact they had rushed into a marriage.

Can you believe -- they never celebrated their wedding anniversary? I don't even know their marriage date. They never talked about it.

I only found out about the feared pregnancy much later as an adult. Looking back, I wondered about their feelings. Even though they loved each other, I felt their guilt.

I always said, "Guilt didn't run in our family, it galloped." That's because lots of things didn't get talked about in our family.

After they got married, my mom and dad moved to Lapaz, Indiana, where they opened a little grocery store. Six years later, in 1940, my father's father passed away. My parents moved back to my dad's family house to live with my grandmother.

When World War II broke out, my dad was 30 years old. By this time, my parents had a daughter and a new baby boy. To support the war effort, my father started working at Kingsbury Munitions Plant, as a guard in Westville, Indiana.

It wasn't long before the family grew. I came along in 1943. Then a sister arrived in 1944, another sister in 1946, and my younger brother in 1948.

Imagine. Six of us kids were born from April,1940 to October 1948. All six with my grandmother, father and mother living together in a little farmhouse.

I'm sure it was challenging for my mother. She was just busy, trying to do her best. But what happened to me as a toddler turned my life upside down. It became a significant emotional upheaval, a major event in my life.

When my mom gave birth to my sister, just 21 months younger than me, she turned my care over to my father's mother. My grandmother became my primary caregiver.

As I look back, I know my mother was tending to my older brother, my sister and a younger sister, and she needed help in caring for so many children. I'm sure she had no idea what impact it would have on me.

But suddenly, I felt abandoned by my mother. As a kid, I felt like I didn't belong. I believed I wasn't worth much.

Why didn't my mother want to raise me like the others in the family?

Why ME? Did I do something wrong?

REFLECTIONS

1. What were the circumstances around your parents' courtship and wedding?

2. Are you aware of any friction between families?

3. If you have siblings, how do you feel your position in the family has affected your feelings about yourself? If you are an only child or an adopted child, how has that made a difference in your outlook?

4. What is your earliest concern or memory during your childhood that still affects you as an adult?

CHAPTER 3
What Happens In Early Childhood Stays With You

Even as a grownup, that first traumatic event of being abandoned by my mother still troubled me. I had to understand more. As an adult, I finally asked my mother the big "WHY" question.

"Why did you tell grandma to raise me?"

My mother paused as she looked into my eyes. "Your grandmother loved you," she simply said. "She especially liked you because you looked a lot like your dad."

"What, you didn't love me?" I said.

Being raised by my grandmother became a huge event in how I shaped my sense of self. I learned that we begin to develop our concept of ourselves and the world around us early in life. While I loved my grandmother, she wasn't my mother. She was a nice woman, but she acted very stoic and didn't say much. She looked after me, and later, it was my job to look after her.

Being aware that I was different from my siblings led me towards forming an early sense of independence. My grandmother told me about one amusing event when I was three or four. One day, I started pulling my wagon toward the road in front of our house.

"Where are you going?" My grandmother asked, watching me closely.

"I am going to see the world," was my quick reply. She had to stop me. I wanted to explore at an early age, and that feeling continues now.

As I grew up on the farm, there were always chores to be done. It was a 100-acre vegetable farm! When I was five years old, I started working for my uncle, 15 hours a week, weeding vegetables and harvesting them. When I got a little older, I helped at the Farmers Market in South Bend.

At age 12 or 13, when I got big enough, I began working for my father on rooftops. My father had started a roofing, insulation and siding company after the war was over, and I worked for him during the summers until I went to graduate school.

Working on the farm and on the roofs taught me a lot. The biggest thing I learned was -- I didn't want to work that hard when I grew up! Doing hard labor convinced me to stay in school and get a good education. I've always worked hard, but I didn't want to physically endure so many challenges.

Another big factor that shaped my sense of self was my older brother. I hate to admit it, but my older brother and I grew up hating each other.

I do not know why he had such animosity toward me, but he did. Every day, he would physically pick on me or make fun of me. He even recruited his two friends to help him do it. My only ally was my cousin, Gene, and unfortunately, he was not a good fighter.

My mother would admonish us, "Go outside if you're going to fight!" But I never wanted to do that. I knew what was going to happen outside. It was not going to be pleasant... and I was going to suffer.

To cope with the harassment, I learned it was best to hide my feelings. I didn't want to show my brother that I was upset because it only made the situation worse. My feelings stayed pent up inside.

It took years until the physical intimidation finally stopped. And it stopped for only one reason. After my freshman year in high school, I grew six inches. Suddenly, I became bigger than my brother!

One day, when he started picking on me, I picked him up and dropped him on his head! He was shocked. After that, though he stopped his physical abuse, he continued to shame me. I call it, "guilt tripping." He had a way of making me feel guilty for anything that I was involved with.

It was a strange experience growing up in our family. On the surface, everything looked normal and happy. Underneath, there was upset and confusion. No one knew.

We all had an image of how the family should be, and naturally, we publicly played the role. We acted like the perfect family, but we definitely weren't the perfect family...

REFLECTIONS

1. What influential person or people played a key role in shaping your life?
2. What question or concern has been left unsaid?
3. What perceptions did you have in early childhood about yourself?   Have you been able to resolve any issues at this point in time?
4. How did you handle conflict between family members?
5. Have you been able to share your feelings as an adult with them?   If someone is not alive, you can still speak to their spirit.

CHAPTER 4
Life Behind the Scenes On The Farm

While I faced many challenges in my youth, growing up on my family's farm also provided lots of positive experiences. I especially loved where we lived.

Picture two homes -- one with my aunt, uncle and three cousins living next door, and our home on a 100-acre vegetable farm. My cousin Gene was one of my best friends. We had great fun hanging out together. Our farm bordered a lake with five acres of woods. As we grew up, we got to explore and play freely in this rural, natural setting.

There was a community around the lake, with lots of kids to play with. We would swim, fish, play sports, go bike riding, and hunt turtles and frogs. We went hunting in the winter, ice skating, and built tree houses. We searched for Indian beads and arrow heads.

Ah -- we were free to do so many things! Best of all, we could roam and explore without much supervision because it was safe.

In the morning, I would say goodbye to my grandmother and mother, and then off I went! Sometimes, I didn't see them until dinner.

I knew people loved each other in the family. I loved them too, even though I hated my brother every day. However, we never expressed our love for each other. For that matter, we never expressed any feelings for each other, other than anger.

Looking back, I wish we could have shared our feelings with each other. It would have given us peace of mind.

Having Pets Wasn't Easy

Growing up around nature could have been an idyllic situation. But it wasn't. Especially when I remember how our pets were treated.

I believe every experience provides a lesson. Yet one of my hardest lessons revolved around our pets. I had to suppress my feelings around them, because I loved our pets so much. They were my buddies. But not everyone in my family felt the same way. Especially my father. He just saw animals as commodities. Here today, gone tomorrow.

Let me tell you about my pet chicken. When I was about five years old, I became attached to one of the chickens we were raising. I called him, "Jimmy."

I *really* liked Jimmy. I think he liked me too. I could pick out Jimmy from the rest of the chickens. He was my favorite.

One day, my dad needed to take some chickens to be killed for our food. He had to try to catch enough to be slaughtered which was not easy, and he happened to catch Jimmy. I watched him carefully and called out.

"Dad, you caught Jimmy!" My heart was beating fast.

Do you know what he told me? He denied it. "No, that's not Jimmy," he said. He was frustrated because it was so hard to catch enough.

I KNEW it was Jimmy. But it didn't matter. My father took him away. Away to be killed for us to eat.

AAAUUUGGHHHH! How could he do that?

"Jimmy was gone," I told myself, pushing down my hurt, my upset, my pain. I felt I didn't matter. Why would he take Jimmy? My feelings meant nothing to my father. I began to think it was best not to feel anything.

Having to suppress my feelings extended to our dogs. Growing up, we always had a dog. But I also had to learn not to get too attached to them. Unfortunately, I never knew how long they'd stay alive in our home.

We never kept our dogs tied up. Sometimes, they would get killed on the road by cars passing in front of our house. Other times, my dad took our dogs to the woods, and shot them with the shotgun. (Yes, you heard me right!) He did it just because they happened to get into the chicken coop and killed a chicken.

"Once they get the taste of a chicken," my father sternly proclaimed, "they will keep going after them." Whatever my father decided was final. When he felt he needed to get rid of those dogs, that was it. No discussion.

I'll never forget our dog Trixie. She was such a sweetheart. When I was 10 or 11, my cousin and I were walking six miles into town. Our dog, Trixie trotted beside us, without a leash. As we walked, Trixie ran out onto the road, just as a car was speeding by.

I watched the car hit Trixie and never stop. Trixie ended up in the ditch and as I rushed to her side, she died. I felt terribly guilty.

Why didn't I watch out for her? Why? WHY? I loved Trixie. In my mind, I felt it was all my fault. I didn't talk to anyone about it, but I still remember it almost seventy years later.

How did I deal with this grief? I kept it inside. I tried to pretend it didn't bother me.

My experience with animals contributed towards the way I shut down my feelings. From a young age, I learned it was too painful to express how I felt. Better to be stoic, like my father. I shouldn't show any weakness. No one should see how I felt inside.

Better to Be A Guest

Certain things were expected of us. We were expected to work hard on the farm and around the house. We always had chores to do. We were also expected to be good students and bring home good grades. So, I did that for the most part.

Even though our old farmhouse didn't have much room, our

friends seemed to enjoy coming over. There always seemed to be extra kids around.

I thought it was better to be a guest of our family than a member. Our guests were always treated very well. There would be sleepovers, especially on the weekends. My sisters always hosted slumber parties.

My cousin, Gene, was at our house more than he was at his. His sisters were much older than him and he felt like an only child. It wasn't much fun for him there. He and I were always hanging out. I would miss him in the winter months, as my aunt and uncle would go to Florida for at least three months and take him with them.

When Gene was gone, there wasn't much to do on the farm and my dad's work would slow down a bit. So, my dad would take over for my uncle at the farmers market in South Bend on Tuesdays, Thursdays and Saturdays.

On Saturdays, I would often have to go to market with my dad to help. Those were long cold days. When I was in junior high school, I had a big run in with my dad over the Christmas break. I'll never forget it.

"I need you to work at the market on Saturday," he said in his strong voice.

"Dad, I have other plans," I answered. I rarely asserted myself, and I really did have a social plan already scheduled.

My father wouldn't take any objection. He immediately began

to guilt trip me. Rather than explain why it was important for me to help him, he did something very hurtful. My parents had given me an early Christmas present that year. It was a nice, winter coat that I needed.

To push me into working with him, he said, "O.K., I guess we can take that coat back if you don't want to help."

What could I say? I really needed that coat!

I went to the market and held a grudge from then on. I learned it was best not to want anything. Otherwise, my wishes could be used to control me. Besides that, my dad had a disapproving look that could pierce my very soul. I still remember the feeling.

My dad worked hard to support our large family. He built up his business, but I don't think he was the best at being a businessman. Unlike his older brothers, he didn't plan well. He tended to be impulsive. He didn't think things through before acting. He also seemed to have problems collecting what was owed him.

That was one of a few things my father and mother fought about. Even though they rarely fought in front of us, I knew that was one thing they disagreed on. My father got up early to start work, and often would have to go out at night to give estimates to potential customers.

When my father returned home, my mother would say, "Don't bother your father. He is tired."

My dad's negative outlook hung over me like a cloud. I remember him saying, "Bob, enjoy it as a kid, because it is miserable as an adult."

"I am already miserable," I thought. "And if it gets worse than this, I should kill myself right now and get it over with."

So being miserable was something that I considered to be inevitable.

REFLECTIONS

1. How comfortable was it to express your feelings in your family?
2. From your family, who was your greatest influence (positive or negative) and why?
3. How significant were pets in your life, and in what way?
4. How would you evaluate your experience as a child?
5. If you had siblings, how did they affect your feelings about yourself?

CHAPTER 5
Not Everything Was Miserable

We all remember good and bad stuff from our youth. Then it's up to us to choose how to put those experiences into a framework. As adults, we can step back, reflect on what happened, and consider what lessons we're supposed to learn.

I certainly had my share of lessons in growing up. Let me start with some of the good times. While my father was an expert at making us feel guilty, he did pass along something I still love -- fishing! What fun it was for all of us kids to go fishing on our lake together.

We kept father so busy that he never got much of a chance to fish. He had to keep baiting our hooks and untangling our lines. But these efforts paid off.

We caught small fish -- perch, bluegill and crappie -- and occasionally caught a catfish. We'd bring the fish home, clean them and fry them up for dinner.

I fell in love with fishing because of those Sundays, and because of my mother's mother also loved fishing. She took us fishing too during our summer visits to her house.

Another favorite memory was playing basketball. Being raised in Indiana, I think they inject you with a love of basketball as a baby and make you addicted to it. We did whatever we could to play at all times of year.

Our garage had a backboard and rim, and that's all we needed to play. However, the driveway was gravel, and it was hard to dribble. We did the best we could. But come winter, we couldn't play outside. I was so frustrated. I had to figure out a solution…. And I did!

At the age of 10, I noticed our hayloft in the barn wasn't being used for anything. It was full of junk.

"Hey, this would make a great indoor basketball court," I said to my dad and older brother. "Would you help me fix it up?"

I enlisted my dad and brother to help me clear it out, and before I knew it, we were putting up backboards and rims. One backboard was an old oak tabletop. The other was some pine boards that we framed into a square. They did the job. I was thrilled. The only problem was that one side of the loft was open. I didn't think it would matter. Boy I was wrong…

One day, while playing basketball with neighbors, one of our friends, Jerry Hummel, did a fade away jump shot and suddenly disappeared. Where did he go? We peered down from the loft, and there was Jerry! Spread eagled on a pile of my dad's warehoused shingles.

Luckily, Jerry wasn't hurt, simply scared. Whew! Our group decided we needed to put up a fence. Soon, our court was safe. Before long, we attracted kids from all over the county to play in our barn.

It was real barn ball. Nothing was out of bounds unless the ball went over the fence. You also had to call your own fouls, but you better be bleeding if you did that. Otherwise, you were considered a wimp.

We were a lively, dedicated group. There were twenty to thirty guys who played regularly. When my younger brother turned five, he wanted to play with us too. We told him he could play if he didn't cry. He became a tough ball player. In the winter, we'd play even when it was cold. Sometimes, we'd play until 1:00 am on a Friday or Saturday night. We had lights but no heat. We had to bounce the ball hard, just to get it warmed up enough to bounce.

But we didn't care how cold it got. At least we were inside with no wind and playing our favorite sport. I loved it! Now at 78 years old, I still play full court basketball with friends, arriving at a gym by 6:00 am on Thursday mornings.

So, you see? Not everything was miserable about my growing up.

Unfortunately, I couldn't play basketball as much as I wanted. That's because my parents expected us to attend Saturday morning Catechism.

During my 5th and 6th grades, Catechism conflicted with basketball practice. So, I had to miss practicing my favorite sport. It set me back in my basketball skills compared to my classmates. I got to be on the team but wouldn't get to play much.

Even though my father didn't profess any religion, my Catholic mother wanted to make sure we learned all the dogma and rules. What bothered me was that it seemed like almost everything was a sin.

I resented having to attend Catechism. I also felt guilty all the time because I felt like a sinner. Being angry was a sin. I was always angry at my brother. That meant I was a sinner.

I would go to confession, relating how many times I was angry with my brother. I'd promise not to be angry in the future. But I knew I'd be angry again. Plus, I was told that having sexual thoughts was a sin. That added to my guilt. Guilt. Guilt. Guilt!

Oh God, how could I live with so much guilt?

Many years later, my brother asked me, "Did you feel guilty as a kid?"

"All the time!" I exclaimed. "Sometimes, I would feel guilty and didn't not even know *why* I was guilty!"

"I felt guilty all the time too," my brother later confessed. "Did you get that look from dad?" He grimaced at the memory.

I knew what he meant. That look burned a hole in your soul. Now, decades later, we can talk about it. Both positive and negative influences were shaping my sense of self. And through it all, I was building a wall around my emotions.

CHAPTER 6
Unexpected Traumas

In the 8th grade, two major traumas happened that deeply affected my life.

First, I really liked this girl in my class named Sandra. To my delight, I found out she liked me. I felt elated! I couldn't stop smiling. The two of us attended a high school basketball game and sat next to each other. At the game, I put my arm around her. At half-time we went outside, and I got my first kiss. I was in bliss. It was wonderful!

My parents were attending the game and were watching me. They saw me with my arm around Sandra. I would soon get the big guilt trip for that!

After the game, there was a school dance for us kids. My dad was a chaperone for the dance. When I saw my dad at the dance, he gave me the **Look.**

Oh NO! I knew he had seen me with Sandra. I shriveled up inside and felt so guilty. Guilt, Guilt, GUILT!

With that one look, I went from ecstasy to agony. I so much wanted my dad's approval. But how could I get it? I was devastated to see his disapproval. He never even talked to me about his concerns.

I couldn't take it. I stopped hanging out with Sandra and never told her why. I still feel badly about that.

The next thing that happened really knocked me in the gut. BIG time!

I had a lot of friends in my class, but other than my cousin, Gene, Nelson Huff was my best friend. We were in classes together, played sports with each other, were in the school band together and hung out whenever we had a chance. There was no one like Nelson.

Nelson was a happy-go-lucky kid, who was friendly to everyone. We laughed and joked, and just enjoyed each other. He was a prankster too, so we had great fun together.

One day, just before lunch, we were in band class together. When band class was over, we ran outside, taking a short cut to the cafeteria, so we could be first in line. It was very cold out, but we didn't care. We ran to the cafeteria without our coats on.

Entering the warm cafeteria, we proceeded through the line to get our food. Then, the unbelievable event happened. An event that's forever imprinted into my memory. As we walked to our table, Nelson was in front of me. Suddenly, Nelson dropped his tray and fell on the floor. He just lay there, and within moments, he began turning blue.

"Nelson!" I cried out. I was shocked! I didn't know what to do. Other students stood back, staring at us.

My best friend, Nelson was passing away right in front of me. His heart stopped. The electrical signals that keep the heart pumping had stopped. My own heart felt like it wanted to stop too.

I was helpless. I wondered for the longest time whether our running out into the cold and then back into the heated cafeteria had caused his heart to stop. I have no idea.

Back then, we didn't know CPR, or we might have been able to save him. How could I possibly process this emotional upheaval? I felt overwhelmingly sad, terrified, and even angry at Nelson's loss.

I couldn't believe Nelson could be so vibrant at one moment, and then gone in an instant. I couldn't cry. I couldn't make myself attend his funeral. It was just too much pain to bear.

I still miss Nelson, and always will.

REFLECTIONS

1. What was your earliest memory of someone's passing who was close to you? How did it affect you?
2. What does death mean to you?
3. How have you handled losses you have experienced?
4. Have you gotten support?
5. How does your family deal with loss?

CHAPTER 7
Escape To The Seminary

After being traumatized in 8th grade, I didn't know what to do next. Somehow, I came up with the idea of going to the seminary and studying to be a priest.

I don't know all the reasons. Perhaps it was my father's scathing look. Or Nelson's sudden death. Or the fact that I had no one to confide in.

I was really shook up. Death scared me. I didn't have my parents' approval to like girls. My buddy was gone. What could I do? I was confused and lost.

I didn't want to die and go to hell. I thought that becoming a priest seemed like a good idea. Plus, I was tired of working all the time, and it seemed to me that priests only worked on Sundays. From my viewpoint, people gave money to priests, and they had a prestigious position. I might even feel like I mattered. I concluded the seminary was the right place for me.

So, I told my parents I wanted to apply for it. They reluctantly agreed. I was the first from our family and parish to go to the seminary. I'm sure I felt some thrill to be the first, but that thrill was short lived.

Within two days of being at the seminary, I knew I didn't want to be there.

Here I was -- at a picturesque setting, Our Lady of the Lake Seminary, on Lake Wawasee, in Syracuse, Indiana. And I didn't know what to do. I was housed at a converted hotel, which had its heyday during the time of prohibition. While it was known for its gambling and prostitution, frequented by Al Capone, its evolution into becoming a seminary created quite a contrast.

The seminary was a diocesan minor seminary, with Crosier priests doing the teaching. It was called a minor seminary because it taught boys in high school and their first two years of college. Students stayed at the seminary for the school year, with a few days at home for Thanksgiving, Christmas vacation and Easter week. We got three months off for summer vacation. Our parents could visit once a month for a few hours on a Sunday afternoon. I was living in a different reality, and I knew I didn't belong there.

We studied a lot, went to chapel several times a day, including daily mass. On Sundays, we attended Mass twice. We had classes every day but Sunday. We had half a day off on Saturdays for free time in the afternoon. We still had study hall in the evening. Sundays we would have the afternoons free and a few hours in the evening.

I missed my family and didn't want to be there, but I said nothing about that as I was told if I left the seminary I would surely go to hell. My spiritual director told me that I had a vocation and if I turned my back on it, I would be disappointing God and probably end up in hell. I believed what he said so I stayed in my own created prison. I was miserable.

When I was around 20 and still in the minor seminary, another tragedy occurred. My cousin, Gene, whom I had been closest to, was killed in an automobile accident.

I was one of his six pallbearers. The funeral was quiet, not much was said. I don't recall if there was even a eulogy. The minister said a few words at the cemetery, and no one else spoke.

As his casket was lowered, I didn't feel anything. I didn't cry or feel sad. At the time, I thought it was strange that I didn't feel anything.

I wondered, "Am I just this non-feeling person who doesn't care?" That thought bothered me. Looking around the faces of family and friends, that same stoic attitude pervaded our sacred space. Everyone's eyes were downcast. I saw my uncle Roy, my cousin's father, not shed one tear, and not even talking about his own son. I'm just like him, I thought. How awful! But I didn't know what to do about it.

After the funeral, my parents had a gathering at our house. I was struck by the fact that as my uncle talked with different people, his words were about business. I don't recall him even mentioning his son. No one was crying.

Coming back to the minor seminary, I had really shut down. I was going through the motions of life.

As a result, I spent six years in the minor seminary, and then another four months in the major seminary, not wanting to be there.

I pretended like I wanted to be there. The worst times were from Christmas to Easter. That time period seemed to take forever and there was very little to do that was fun. I remember having stomach aches often from missing my family. I wanted to go back home, and I wanted to play high school football, but that didn't happen. I wanted to date and that wasn't allowed. I did make some good friends while I was at the seminary, and at times, we would enjoy ourselves. Most of the time was spent going to church, studying and frequently being on kitchen duty. Not fun.

When one of my fellow students would leave the seminary, we didn't get to say goodbye to them. The priests didn't want us to think about leaving. They depicted those departing students as bad people because the students chose to leave. One day certain students would be there, and the next day, they'd be gone. I don't know how others felt. But for me, it was horrible. I'd have friends for several years, and then, it was like they didn't exist anymore. What should I do?

I lived in my own self-created prison, walled in by my beliefs. I felt like if I left, I would be a big sinner, and destined for hell. And who wants to go to hell? Not me. So, I stayed on, graduating from the minor seminary in 1963, with a Liberal Art's Associate Degree.

The bishop decided where we would go next. I didn't feel I had a choice about the direction in my life. It was determined by other people. I was sent in the Fall of 1963 to St. Mary's, a major seminary in Baltimore, Maryland. In the seminary, students were supposed to study philosophy for two years, and then four years of theology before they would be ordained a priest.

Though I had become accustomed to suppressing my feelings, I remember one time when my heart opened. It was on November 22nd, 1963, the day that President John F. Kennedy was killed. I was playing flag football with a group of students, having fun and enjoying getting away from my usual strict schedule inside the seminary. When we heard the news that Kennedy had been shot, I was shocked and upset. It felt like the world had stopped. As I walked with the others inside, we then learned Kennedy had died.

Sadness overcame my senses. It was a new wave of emotion for me, and I allowed myself to feel deeply over the loss of our President. Not only did I have a great deal of respect for Kennedy, but others around me grieved too. For once, I felt I had permission to let that sadness out.

Kennedy's assassination happened right before Thanksgiving, and I was invited to another seminarian's house during that time. Together, we traveled quietly to the gravesite of John F. Kennedy. Walking across the bridge over the Potomac River, I remember getting blisters from my new shoes. Even with that foot pain and the wave of grief surrounding us, I still shed no tears. They just didn't come out.

After the break, I returned to the seminary, and resumed meeting regularly with my spiritual director, Father Geno Walsh. I was lucky to be assigned to him. Father Walsh was a particularly good man. He took the time to get to know me and we became friends. One day, he asked if I wanted to be there.

"I don't get the sense you *really* want to be here," he said thoughtfully.

How could he know what was in my heart? I looked at him, straight in the eyes, and decided to reveal my secret.

"No, I don't want to be here." My heart quickened, as I sensed a sudden crack in the prison door of my life.

"Then why are you here?" He paused, looking deeply at me. It felt so natural, like two friends talking together.

I felt I could open up to Father Walsh, so I continued. "No one ever asked me that before. I'm afraid to leave because I don't want to go to hell. My spiritual directors have always told me I'd go to hell if I left." I believed every word that I was saying.

Father Walsh laughed. "That's nonsense! You should leave if you don't want to be here."

I felt a ton of weight lifting off my shoulders. "I will!" I declared. My prison door flew wide open. What a relief.

I was FREE! Free to do what I wanted to do. Free for the first time in years! Once the semester was over, I left. Free at last! I've been grateful to that man ever since.

I felt so happy, ready to embark on the next part of my life. What might be ahead? What would I do? Where would I go?

For the first time, I felt like I had a choice in my life.

REFLECTIONS

1. How many times have you taken on a direction in your life because you thought you should rather than what you really wanted to pursue?
2. What role has your religion played in your life?
3. Who has influenced you about your beliefs in either a positive or negative way?
4. Have your beliefs about religion or spirituality changed over the years?

CHAPTER 8
What Did I Want?

For the first time, a sense of freedom surrounded me.

Finally, I was out of my self-imposed jail. As I left the seminary, I realized I still had no real direction. I was like a leaf in the wind. I really didn't know how to find myself. How could I suddenly figure out my life's direction?

I was not prepared at all.

While I considered what I wanted to do, I thought about getting a job. But what job would I take? How was I supposed to figure this out? I wasn't used to making my own decisions. It was easier to defer to others. I had ended up allowing my parents to direct my life, without reflecting on any of my own interests. My own passions had been hidden inside for so long. How would I move forward?

My parents were adamant about continuing my education.

I can still hear them. "You need to go on to graduate from college. We don't want you to stop." They were afraid if I got a job I would never go back to school. They told me that if I continued in college, they'd help me with the next semester financially.

I had no money. No idea of future careers. What I really wanted to do was play tackle football. It would cost $900 for the college semester. I didn't know how I felt about other things, but football was the one thing I knew I loved. I missed it when I was at the seminary because they didn't have tackle football.

I considered attending St. Joseph's College in Rensselaer, Indiana, because I thought they might give me that chance to play football.

From working on roofs with my father, I knew I was in great shape. My friends told me that St. Joe's had a lousy football team, so I thought I could make the team in my senior year, and then play at least a year of tackle football. The downside of going to St. Joe's was that it was an all-male school other than a few daytime co-eds.

At that point, all I cared about was playing football. So, I made the decision to go to St. Joe's, solely based on wanting to play football. I didn't even know for sure if they would take me. They did!

I was in for a huge disappointment. When I went out for spring football practice, preparing to get my uniform, they told me I couldn't play in the fall. I'd have to sit out a year because I was a transfer student! What?

I couldn't believe it! Here I was at a school in the middle of the cornfields of Indiana, where you could smell cow manure whenever the wind blew, and it blew a lot. But I couldn't play college football. What was worse, there were no women around. If you wanted to date at all, you had to leave campus to find women.

That was it for me. I decided to leave St. Joe's after that spring semester and transfer to a school that was co-ed.

But even that didn't happen. I did well academically, and the school ended up offering me an academic scholarship, along with a student loan that paid for all of the following year. So, I stayed. I was not too happy about the decision, but economically it made sense. I didn't have the money to go elsewhere.

After the seminary, I realized I was way behind others of my age when it came to meeting, dating and relating to the opposite sex. I was shy and naïve. One of the first dates I had was with a high school girl.

"Aren't you old for that girl?" my mother asked, raising her eyebrows.

"Mom, I may be older, but she is *way* ahead of me socially," I said.

I was interested in dating, but at the same time, I felt extremely nervous. I didn't know how to date. How do you get a girl interested? What should I say or do? I decided to make an effort and tried meeting women whenever I could. Before I knew it, my efforts paid off. I started having several dates. It was fun to finally go out.

Toward the end of the first semester at St. Joe's, I went to a co-ed gathering in Chicago, where Mundelein College was joining up with students from St. Joe's. I got the chance to meet different women, including Florence Morrisey. We danced and talked a bit, as I did with others. I didn't think too much more about it until later.

Soon afterwards, Florence sent me a note. In her own handwriting, she clearly indicated that she liked meeting me. What a surprise!

Me? I had no idea whether women would be attracted to me. But she was! I was thrilled. Though I wasn't particularly attracted to her physically, it was exciting to think that a woman would find me appealing.

Naturally, I wrote back. We started seeing each other off and on. I liked the fact that she liked me. At the same time, I continued to date other women. I don't recall when I started dating her exclusively. It was some time in my senior year. I know I took her to Prom that year.

Upon graduation, I decided to go into the Peace Corps. I eagerly looked forward to that possibility. At the same time, the idea of going to a foreign land for two years scared me. I was accepted. What should I do?

But here again, the decision about my life seemed to be decided by someone else. At that time, Florence got upset about the idea of my absence for two years. We were dating exclusively then.

What was I to do? I was always trained to be nice. I didn't want to upset anyone. If my mother told me once to be nice, she told me a thousand times... "Be Nice!" That was the worst advice I had ever gotten. I was supposed to please others and ignore how I felt.

Naturally, I changed my mind about the Peace Corps. All because I had to please Florence.

I allowed Florence to influence me into changing my mind. In my thinking, what Florence wanted was more important than what I wanted. That was the pattern I had already set since childhood.

Viet Nam was really heating up at that time. Since I wasn't going to the Peace Corps, I needed to figure out my next step. I considered either joining the military or going to school. What should I do?

Instead of putting my interests first, I again reached out to Florence, and wanted to please her. What do you think she wanted? (If you've guessed going to school, you're right.)

Since Florence was going to teach in Des Plaines, Illinois, I applied for graduate studies in social work at University of Illinois (Chicago campus), Loyola and the University of Chicago. I got fellowship offers from all three schools.

Graduate school allowed me to have a student deferment from the military while I was a student. I decided on the University of Illinois, because Loyola was a Catholic school and I had enough with Catholic education. The University of Chicago focused on social administration and policy, and that didn't interest me. They also wanted my commitment to work for two years after graduation at the Illinois Juvenile Research organization. There was no such obligation with the fellowship from the University of Illinois. So off I went!

Our feelings give us direction in life and tell us what we want. Since I had shut down my feelings long ago, I shut down my important guide.

REFLECTIONS

1. Have you ever felt a lack of direction? Or have you ever felt like others are directing your life?
2. Did you feel you had a choice about what you wanted to do in your life?
3. How did you decide where you wanted to live?
4. Did you ever feel lost in your life? What did you do about it?

CHAPTER 9
Tell Me What to Do

As I look back on my life, I realize how I pleased others at my expense. I didn't know how to make my own decisions! Since Florence wanted me to attend graduate school, that was the direction I chose.

When I moved to Chicago for graduate school, I first lived at a YMCA for several weeks. What an experience!

The room was small and very bleak. It was also kind of scary. Next, I moved into a furnished one-bedroom apartment with another student. He claimed the bedroom and I got the couch. (Again, I was pleasing him!)

That first place didn't last long. We moved again because the original apartment had bugs and the management wouldn't do anything about them. Our next place was a two-bedroom furnished apartment, and we added another roommate. At least this time, I got one of the bedrooms. The new roommate got the couch!

Going to graduate school was not much fun. I struggled through it. I wasn't inspired. I went to classes three days a week and had a field placement two days a week. I worked with foster children at Cook County Public Aid, Children's Division, and wasn't truly clear on my role. Still, I did my best.

The Fellowship paid for my tuition, and I had $200 a month to live on. Back in 1965, $200 was more than it is now, but it still wasn't a lot of money. I was just getting by, and often ate only one meal a day. To make ends meet, I ended up needing to get a part-time job at the Chicago Tribune. I think I was making $1.65 an hour, but it helped.

As for my relationship with Florence, I felt the need to be a good Catholic boy. I knew Florence liked me, and I wanted to be able to have sex. In order to do that, I thought you had to be married. No one told me anything different. I also thought I'd be happy if I could have sex. So that's the bargain I went for.

I believed my job was to please Florence, and I think her job was to be pleased. Both of us were naive. As an only child, she grew up expecting people to take care of her. In my upbringing, I grew up taking care of people. So, we fit well together with our expectations.

It wasn't long before we got married. In August 1966, as we moved into our apartment in Des Plaines, Illinois, I was in for a major disappointment. I wasn't terribly happy! Getting married just didn't make me happy.

Sex with Florence wasn't exactly what I thought it would be. She was very prudish, and our sex life was extremely limited. My hopes for a thrilling relationship crumbled. Was this going to be my life?

To cope with the disappointment, I started putting on weight like mad. I needed to give myself some satisfaction. As I look back, I know I didn't realize at the time why I kept overeating. I had shut my feelings down. I just did what I had to do each day. As the years passed, I gained at least 100 pounds. I was going through the motions of life, without knowing what I really wanted.

Florence had gotten a job in Niles, less than a half a mile from our apartment. We had one car between us. I had to travel into Chicago to school and then to my second-year field placement at Presbyterian St. Luke's Hospital in their outpatient psychiatric clinic.

You'd think Florence would have given me the car. It would have been much easier for her to get a ride from her friends who taught at her school, because her work was so close. But that's not what happened. Florence wanted the car. Again, I thought my job was to please her for whatever she wanted.

So, guess who drove the car? Florence! Her job was five minutes away. I had to take public transportation into Chicago five days a week. It took me at least an hour and a half each way every day. What an exhausting trip! But did I say anything about it? No. I was a good victim.

On Christmas Eve, just four months after our marriage, I got a letter from the draft board to report for a physical. Previously, I had considered going into the service. But Florence in no way wanted me to go. When I went for the physical, I thought I'd be going into the army after graduation.

The draft board ended up saying, "You have ingrown toenails… and that disqualifies you."

Can you believe that? Ingrown toenails disqualified me! I think they were afraid I'd get gangrene if I got into the service. My face must have registered my surprise.

Trying to make me feel better, a draft officer said, "Look, if you have surgery on your toenails and get them healed, we'll take you."

Then, I was called upon again. The draft board had me back for another physical, and I failed again. Twice, I had to get doctors' notes that I had ingrown toenails. The draft board was desperate to get me in, but I just didn't make it. I put off surgery on my toenails until I was 30 at Florence's urging.

Afterwards, I had many mixed feelings. Friends of mine were in service. Some of my friends were killed in Vietnam. I didn't agree with the war, but at the same time, I felt you're supposed to serve your country. What did I want to do? I figured out the answer.

I knew I didn't want to be killed. So, I never served in the army.

REFLECTIONS

1. How skilled did you feel about dating?
2. If you got married, how did you decide on your spouse being the right person to marry?

3. If you have a significant relationship, how easily do you feel you can openly talk to each other?

4. On a scale of 1-10, how satisfying is your relationship and why?

CHAPTER 10
It Shouldn't Have Happened

Not quite two years after I got married, I experienced another tragedy.

My dad was working on a roof, and he accidentally fell off. I'm not sure exactly how it happened, but I know where he got hurt. He hit a concrete stoop, and unfortunately, he crushed the bones in his chest. I'm sure he was in terrible pain. He got rushed by ambulance to the hospital in Mishawaka, Indiana.

My mother called to let me know about the accident, and explained that dad had been working alone. As he neared the roof's edge, he somehow slipped off. When he was in a rush, he often took risks that he probably shouldn't have done. He had other accidents because he would be in a rush, but none this severe.

At the time, I was working in Chicago. It was in the middle of the week. My mother said it looked like he would recover. We waited until the weekend to go to Mishawaka to the hospital.

Looking at dad, bruised and bandaged in the bed, I kept thinking, "Dad is strong, a hardy soul. He'll get better." His face looked determined to get through this situation. Our family, friends and the doctors were sure he'd recover and survive.

As you know by now, my family didn't talk much about their feelings. But just seeing him lying in the hospital bed, I felt so uneasy. I wanted to tell him how much I cared about him. I wanted to be able to hug him… show him I loved him. I had a sense he wanted to share something with me too.

But it didn't happen. He looked at me but couldn't express his feelings. Time ticked by, and it got late. My father probably felt uncomfortable with all of us staring at him, trying to make polite conversation.

"Go home; get some rest," he said, shooing us away. "I'll see you tomorrow." We nodded to him and said our goodbyes before leaving.

Yes, it was obvious father didn't want to talk much. He could have died from that fall. Still, he didn't want to talk about his concerns, his possible death, his love for us. You could feel the tension in the room. No one was expressing what was in their heart. We all learned well how to keep our feelings in check. Repressing our feelings was the norm. No one knew how to open up.

Once we returned to the family house, as we prepared for bed, we barely spoke. Everyone was quite somber. But you could feel the tension.

I stayed with my family that night. Somehow, I made myself close my eyes to get some sleep. At 4am, the phone rang. We all jumped at the sound. I know our nerves were on edge. The call was from the nurse at the hospital.

"He's not doing well," she said with a serious tone. "I think you'd better come."

My heart was pounding. How could that be? He seemed alright when we left him several hours ago. But by the time we got to the hospital, we were informed of the worst news... the unexpected news...

Dad had died! He died alone -- without any of us there. How terrible! How tragic. How could he have died so quickly? What happened? My mind was filled with questions.

I gazed down at him. His face looked peaceful and out of pain. I wondered what caused his sudden death. I just *had* to know.

As we asked around, we found out later that a nurse had given him the wrong medication. He had been hallucinating, walking around the halls of the hospital with a crushed chest. No one knew how much that contributed to his death. But his lungs filled with fluid, and then he drowned from his own fluid. How long was he wandering the halls? How quickly did he pass? Did anyone try to save him?

All kinds of questions arose in my mind. I wanted to sue, but my mother refused. She didn't want to go through the pain of legal proceedings. Inside, I was boiling over.

This was one time I did know how I felt. I was furious that he died. I felt hurt and incredibly heartbroken. I screamed and yelled. My voice sounded haunting, primeval. I was ready to tear the hospital down.

"AAAAAAUUUGGGGHHH!"

I hated feeling helpless. It was so, *so* unfair. My whole family was upset. I was terribly disturbed, devastated, and troubled that I don't really recall any of the family's reactions. I was mainly aware of mine. How could this happen?

At my dad's wake, hundreds of people streamed through the funeral home. They came to be with us, telling me how much my father had done for them. That's where I heard about my dad's impact on people.

I couldn't believe it! Were they talking about my father? I never realized my dad's actions had touched so many lives. He always kept his outreach to others private.

"He was like a second father to me," said at least a dozen men.

"I'm so grateful to your father," said others.

"Your father helped us so much." One person after the next confided their gratitude with us.

So why did they wait so long to let us know? While my father was alive, most people in our community didn't say how they felt. They usually saved their emotions for display at basketball or football games. I don't think any of them ever told my father how they felt about him. That's because they were just like him. Stoic to the core. Keeping everything inside. Now, many of them shared how proud my dad was of me, my brothers and my sisters. Yet, dad never told us himself how proud he was of us.

My dad was quite a giver in the community. A perpetual volunteer for different causes. He served as a volunteer fireman. He raised money for the local hospital. He raised money for the church and helped build it. He belonged to the Kiwanis Club, always doing charitable things. He helped with the Boy Scouts as an adult leader. The exemplary citizen.

How come so many others had such wonderful experiences with my father? Where was he for us most of the time? Why didn't I receive some of that loving attention? I never remember even getting a hug.

The problem was my dad didn't know how to care for himself. He had a hard time expressing his feelings to us kids. I knew he loved me, but he never told me. He just didn't know how. I think he shook my hand once when I graduated from college. Isn't that something?

I did get touched by him, in an offhand way. To save money, he would cut my older brother's hair and my hair. I still love going to the barber and getting my head touched. I get so relaxed that I almost fall asleep. It reminds me of my father's hands.

As I reflected, I kept thinking of the story about my dad and the old van. It was one of the things my father gave me for a short time.

The van needed work. It was leaking oil. That's why my father was generous. "You can have it," he said, handing me the keys. Oh, WOW!

I still vividly remember my excitement. My own van! Isn't that something? I smiled to myself, imagining taking it on fishing trips with my buddies, and then having all of us sleep in it.

Naturally, I wanted to get it fixed. I studied the area of the leak and found a cracked gasket that sealed the valve cover. I could see where the leak was coming from. Somehow, I figured out how to fix it. I felt so proud that I now had a van which ran well.

Well, my joy was short-lived. A few days later, I came home, and the van was gone. "What happened to my van?" I asked, raising my voice to my parents. How could it just disappear?

It turned out that my father decided to be very generous. Generous with MY van! What was most upsetting to me was that he didn't even consider my feelings.

My father acted like nothing was wrong. "Well since it was working, I sold it to a family that needed transportation for $50."

I couldn't believe it. He didn't even ask me ahead of time. He could have said, "Hey, I found this family that really needed transportation. Would it be okay with you if we sell to them?"

No! He just sold it to them, expecting me to be okay with it. You see, my dad was great at putting other people first... before both himself and often us kids. I felt like I could never trust him. I never knew what might happen next.

Many years later, my youngest sister, Carol, went to a Medium to see if she could talk to her husband who had died from cancer.

She was able to talk to him and my grandmothers. Toward the end of the hour, the Medium said that there was a shy man present. It turned out to be my father.

From the Other Side, my father told Carol that he wanted to apologize to us kids. He said that he thought he was being loving towards us, but he didn't realize how his actions hurt our feelings. He came from a family that didn't know how to show love. Dad said he learned a lot since he passed. He wanted us all to know he loved us very much and I wanted to apologize for all the pain he caused us, especially Carol and myself.

"I'm always around," said my father. "You all can talk to me anytime." Now, at last, I feel at peace with my father. As it turns out, I do talk to him all the time.

But at the time of his death, I shut down even more. I was feeling more depressed than ever. Somehow, I managed to function. I did my job. But I was simply going through motions. The pent-up emotions of depression, frustration and anger over losing my father and being in an unhappy marriage got to me.

I didn't know how to handle my feelings, except by eating. Eating gave me some pleasure. The only problem was -- I kept gaining weight.

Before I knew it, I was over 300 pounds. And that's not a healthy situation.

REFLECTIONS

1. How does (or did) your relationship with your mother and father affect your life?
2. Have you dealt with an unexpected death? What helped you cope?
3. What can you do when you're faced with others who don't know how to express their grief?
4. How can you heal when you have so many unresolved emotions after someone passes away?

CHAPTER 11
When My Life Turned Upside Down

Two years after my father died, Florence and I had a beautiful daughter.

Jennifer Marie was born on October 4, 1970, and I was stunned by the feelings that swept over me when I saw her through the nursery window. Wow! She took my breath away! Back then, the doctors didn't let fathers in the delivery room. As I gazed at her, I remember standing at the nursery window crying. Tears flowed, unchecked.

I felt so much love for her. Such a miracle. I could feel how much I loved her through my whole body. I remember thinking, "I wished somebody loved *me* that much." She was so lovely! An angel. And she changed my life.

I was going through changes at my work too. After finishing graduate school, I started working at an outpatient mental health center. From there, I went to work at a hospital. After a couple of years, I started a private practice on the side doing psychotherapy. From the hospital, I then moved on to become chief social worker at an alcoholic treatment center. Busy, busy, busy.

After several years, I heard of a job as an employee counselor for a large pharmaceutical company. I got hired, and the job was so fulfilling. The company had 21,000 employees worldwide, and I was the only counselor.

Can you imagine meeting the needs of so many? My services were in demand. It made me feel wonderful helping employees and their families in person and by phone.

I could see the difference I was making. The lives of employees and their family members were working better. Addictions were overcome, anxiety was diminished, and depression was lifted. Families were solving problems at home and problems at work disappeared. Employees were enjoying life more, improving relationships, being more productive and feeling so much better about themselves.

I even solved business problems such as excessive turnover of female sales representatives and abortive relocations of employees and their families. I really enjoyed developing the scope of counseling. By sheer willpower and determination, I was getting positive results. It was gratifying to hear their feedback.

"Your therapy really made such a difference for me, Bob."

"I don't know how I would have overcome my drinking problem."

"My wife and I feel so much happier together."

"I feel so much better about myself."

At the same time, I was very much out of touch with my own feelings. I had done a great job shutting them down. To do psychotherapy without knowing how *you* feel is quite a hard job. A psychotherapist is supposed to be aware of inner feelings. (That's our expertise, right?)

Ironically, I became more aware of feeling numb to my own inner state. I certainly didn't feel happy. The universe must have known I needed help badly. Perhaps it was my father's spirit who nudged me in the right direction. What happened next was something I never intended for myself, but it was exactly what I needed.

It happened in a very serendipitous way. One of my clients was a woman who was less in touch with her feelings than me. (Imagine that!) I was having trouble making any progress with her. What could I do to help? I decided to find someone with more specialized experience. That led to a therapist who did body psychotherapy.

I still remember calling the therapist, letting him know I needed to refer my client. He threw me a curve ball.

"Why don't *you* come in and let me train you in what I do?" he asked. "Then you can work with her yourself."

"I don't know." I hesitated, worrying that it wouldn't work.

"Just give it a try," he answered with assurance. "I believe in you."

His words intimidated me, but I agreed to take him up on his offer. I never anticipated what I was getting into.

It was TORTURE!

To get me to relax all my tightened muscles from a lifetime of suppressing my feelings, I went through a physical workout. Some exercises made me terribly nauseous. One of the worst was where I had to lean over a small, padded bench backwards. I thought it was going to break my back. Very painful! The muscles in my back were so tight.

The exercises were grueling. I felt sick! SICK! SICK!

I especially dreaded the exercises that involved loosening up my diaphragm and neck. Ugh! Those were especially nauseating. Even entering his waiting room would set off my nausea. My body seemed to know what I was about to do, and obviously, it resisted at every step. Oh, who would have thought my inner anguish would bring up so much physical pain?

While I hated working on my inner self, the benefits began to pay off. I felt a lightness coming from my heart. I became more aware of my feelings. My whole body started feeling lighter. More relaxed. Free. I began eating better and took up running every day.

What do you think happened? I started losing weight, and eventually I lost over 100 pounds! I couldn't believe it. For the first time, I felt more alive.

One of my greatest joys was being around my daughter, Jennifer. I called her Jenny and loved watching her blossom into an exceptionally talented young lady. At age six, when she began playing piano by ear, we got her piano lessons. At the same time, she started taking oil painting lessons, and was a natural at that too. I still have one of her paintings.

Meanwhile, our marriage wasn't going well. Being more in touch with my feelings, I noticed our communication was terrible. Neither of us were happy. We kept having arguments. Nothing felt right. What should we do?

In the spring of 1978, we decided to separate. I moved out and found an apartment in Chicago. Florence and Jenny continued to live in our home in Arlington Heights, Illinois. While Florence and I stayed friendly, both of us started to date. I was working full time at the pharmaceutical company and continued a part-time private practice to support my wife and daughter.

One night in June of 1979, the unexpected happened. The worst possible nightmare. A horrendous tragedy that turned my life upside down.

I was home in my apartment when I got the call. A neighbor in Arlington Heights was on the line.

"Your house caught fire!" There was panic in her voice. *"You've got to get here. Your wife and daughter were burned, and they're being taken to Northwest Community Hospital."*

My heart started pounding like mad. I was shocked and blurted out, *"What? What happened? How badly are they burned?"*

The neighbor didn't know. No matter. I dashed into my car and drove like a wild person to the hospital. All kinds of questions whirled in my mind. How did it happen? What started the fire? Would they be alright?

Twenty long minutes later, as I pulled up into the parking lot and raced inside the emergency room, I was told my wife and daughter were being transferred to the burn unit at Cook County Hospital in Chicago. Two ambulances waited in the driveway -- one for Jenny and one for Florence. They each came out on stretchers, with sheets covering their bodies. Their heads were wrapped in bandages.

My mind was reeling. I couldn't believe what I was seeing. I stood watching in shock as the stretcher carrying my sweet Jenny was lifted into the ambulance. One of the drivers ushered me into the front. I wanted to sit alongside my daughter, but he shook his head.

"Sorry, it's not allowed. You've got to be up front."

I frowned and just nodded. "Can you tell me how badly they were burned?"

The driver didn't know. By his face, I could tell it was a serious situation.

Trembling, I climbed up into the passenger seat. The scene felt surreal. I saw my wife Florence being lifted into the second ambulance. In a minute, the ambulances took off, sirens blaring. We maneuvered our way through traffic, down the highway, with my heart pounding at every turn. Finally, we arrived at Cook County Hospital's emergency room door.

It was the worst ride I've ever taken in my life. The whole time, I kept praying. "Please, please, God. Watch over them. Protect them. Let them be okay."

I still didn't know how badly they were burned.

A nightmare began to unfold. When we got to the burn unit, I was ushered into a waiting room. It seemed like forever before one of the doctors came out to tell me their condition.

He pulled me aside with a grave expression. To my horror, he said, "Your wife has been burned over 60% of her body and your daughter has been burned over 90% of her body. We will do everything possible to save them, but we give them little chance. Infections will set in. That will most likely kill them, because they have so little skin left to protect their body."

The doctor paused, looking at me with concern. I couldn't believe the words I was hearing. I could barely speak.

"Can I see them?" I asked hoarsely. "Would they be able to see or hear me?"

The doctor placed his hand on my shoulder. A small comfort. "Your wife and daughter can hear, but they can't speak or see because of the burns," he said slowly. "You can see them during visiting hours for five minutes every two hours.

My mind was reeling. What? Only five minutes every two hours? Can this be really happening?

"You'll have to wear a hospital gown and mask when you visit. I am deeply sorry to tell you this. My staff is all upset." The doctor grimaced as he noticed my ashen face. "They're finding it very difficult to control their feelings as they work with your family. It's hard for me to tell you this too."

I appreciated his caring manner, but I still couldn't take in the words. I felt like I was going crazy. This could NOT be happening! The doctor shook my hand, and I was left alone, trying to process this catastrophe in my life.

I walked over to the closest reception desk. "When can I see my wife and daughter?" I was told to wait a few minutes. Sitting down in the nearest seat, I looked down at the ground. I didn't know what to do. My world had fallen apart. I was devastated.

Finally, I was told I could go in. Slipping on the hospital gown and mask, I nervously approached their room. What could I possibly say?

Their bodies were wrapped in sterile bandages. Tubes led from a machine into their nostrils. I felt awkward, not knowing what words to say in my brief time with them.

"I love you…. I'm here for you."

Sitting in a seat between each of their bedsides, I noticed that my arms began to ache. I felt terrible about how much they were suffering. I knew Florence was concerned about Jenny, and I didn't know how to console her.

At the hospital, no one told me how the fire started. The Arlington Heights police detectives assigned to the case didn't bother coming to the hospital to check in on my wife, and to see if they could learn anything from her. Instead, they asked me to try to communicate with Florence.

Although Florence couldn't speak, she could make signals for yes and no. I asked questions, and it was clear my wife was frustrated with me. I couldn't figure out what she was trying to tell me. I would find out later that the police knew more than they were telling me.

I had such little time with them. Within three days, my daughter died, and the day after that, my wife died.

We had their funeral a few days later. Family and friends gathered at a cemetery in Des Plaines, looking at me and then away. I could tell by the solemn faces and tears that no one knew what to say. I watched grief-stricken as my beloved daughter and wife's bodies were lowered in a casket into gravesites, side by side. Sobs erupted from me, coming from a dark, unknown space, threatening to overwhelm my body in a tidal wave of grief.

Do you know the saying, "There are no words for how I am feeling?" That's exactly how I felt. No words. No hope. No reason for living.

What the police hadn't told me was that my house had been purposely set on fire. Someone had poured gasoline through the dining room and living room. I found out later that the two detectives had other jobs and didn't want to take the time to come and interview my wife. They wanted to chalk the fire up to the conclusion that my wife attempted suicide.

Of course, I knew that wasn't true. Only after my wife and daughter died, did I find out someone had purposefully set the house on fire. The police suspected I may have done it, and suspected the man whom my wife was dating.

We both had to take lie detectors to prove we weren't involved. I was full of hurt, sadness, rage, hatred and so much more. This was not supposed to happen. Nothing meant anything anymore!

After discovering that someone intentionally set the house on fire, I wanted to find them and kill them with my bare hands. That was the only thing I could think about -- day and night. Night and day.

Even though I was tired, I couldn't sleep. Every day felt like a nightmare. I was agitated, depressed, and ready to die myself. I contemplated killing myself, but I didn't know what to do. I didn't want to suffer. Just go quickly. But first, I had to find out who was behind the arson of our home.

After a few weeks, I even tried going back to work. But by the time I got there, I had to turn around and go back home. I was too weary to work. For two months, I could barely sleep. I would sleep a tiny bit and wake up and be overcome with depression. I cried all the time.

Occasionally, a calm would settle over me. I'd think the fire didn't happen. I imagined I'd go see them. Then reality would hit. My emotional upheaval would take over again.

My arms kept aching. How could I go on living?

REFLECTIONS

1. Have you ever suffered from a huge loss?
2. What happened? How did you feel?
3. What did you do to take care of yourself?
4. Have you ever had to help someone else deal with loss? What did you do?

CHAPTER 12
The Beginning of Recovery

I was in awfully bad shape.

I never thought I would ever be suicidal or homicidal. Well, I was both big time. I was beyond miserable.

About two months after their deaths, I fell into a deep sleep one night and had an amazing dream. I was in this house that had a living room and dining room in the shape of an "L". I was sitting on the floor in the dining room with my back against the wall. To my left was the door to the kitchen. The rooms were completely empty, but it looked like the walls were freshly painted and that there was new carpet. As I was sitting there, someone walked through the kitchen door and handed me a big homemade envelope with drawings on it.

"It's a card from Jenny," I thought.

Then I remembered, "No, Jenny died from a fire."

Another thought popped into my mind. "She must have made it before the fire, and someone just found it."

Sure enough, it *was* a card from Jenny... a Christmas card. It had all her drawings on it. On the inside, the card read, "Merry Christmas, Dad. I love you very much, Jenny."

I woke up crying. After that dream, I could finally sleep again and get rest.

I realized the house was like my life. Empty, with no meaning. I always thought people with meaning would come along, and I would run into them.

But I learned something from that dream. I recognized I'm the one who gives meaning to everything in my life. I'm the creator of meaning. When I give meaning to things and people, I must allow myself to be vulnerable and possibly be hurt. And that's not easy.

Eventually, we all must face loss, at least physically. By allowing ourselves to be open to loss, we must be willing to be brave. It's one of the bravest things we all do as human beings - - to allow ourselves to move on in life after losing a loved one.

After the dream, I knew my daughter was telling me, "Dad, get off your ass and start creating meaning in your life." Her Christmas card was a way of telling me, "Dad, be creative!" She knew that Christmas always meant to me, a time of creation.

Years later, I had a friend who is a medium, and I asked her to talk with my daughter. One of the things I asked was about that dream. Was she responsible for that message?

The medium channeled Jenny, and I got the answer.

"Dad, you were in a terrible place and I needed to help you. Yes, I was responsible for that dream. I stayed close to you for two years because of the difficult place you were in."

The road to recovery was long, but that dream helped me begin to heal. I encountered many ups and downs. Some days, I'd feel better, and on other days, I'd feel worse.

I don't know how it happened, but one day I was feeling so bad that I began wailing. I started making these loud sounds that seemed to come from deep down inside of me. I think I was in my apartment by myself. It was like I was emotionally throwing up. I am sure you have had the experience of physically throwing up. You don't look forward to doing it but when you do you feel so much better. That's how I felt after I wailed the first time.

I was surprised by how much lighter and better I felt. So much pain seemed to be lifted out of me. I never knew when I was going to wail. It would just seem to happen. I would be thinking of something or see something that would bring it on. I don't know how many times I wailed. Many times. Each time I would feel so much better afterward. I found out that there weren't words for what I went through, but there were sounds. Those sounds helped me heal so much.

I didn't know that wailing for my wife and daughter would lead me to wailing for my father, my cousin, and my best friend in 8th grade. When I would get triggered by their memories, I found myself wailing for them.

I had stuffed so much pain around losing them into my body. I carried that pain around for years. What a great relief it was to let my anguish out! I could finally let go of it. I felt a weight lifting off my shoulders.

The body does not know time. It holds onto feelings until you express them. Many people who feel depressed have stuffed their feelings inside for so long that they shut their aliveness down. They become numb, as I did. They have a hard time opening up to their feelings.

It's only by releasing inner traumas that we can start living again.

REFLECTIONS

1. How have you expressed your pain?
2. Have you ever felt depressed?
3. How have you dealt with it? Was it effective?
4. Do you reach out for support when you are down?

CHAPTER 13
Looking for the Murderer

As I was recovering from Jenny's and Florence's deaths, I began looking for the person who killed them. I had to find the murderer!

The police didn't help me. They told me *not* to put out a reward for information leading to the arrest of this person. What? I didn't understand their reasoning. Isn't it their job to solve a crime?

Later, I realized the police didn't want a reward posted. Then, they would have to work. I wasn't going to wait for them to try to help me. I'd find out on my own. I eventually put up a $10,000 reward despite their resistance. No leads came from it.

I talked to everyone I thought might know something about what happened that night. I found out that at the time of the fire's start, Florence was on the phone in the upstairs bedroom, talking to a friend. The friend told me that the dogs were barking, so Florence got off the phone to see what they were barking about.

Florence must have run downstairs, seen the fire, and hurried to the phone in the kitchen to call the fire department. Three days later, the phone was still off the hook. Next, Florence must have run back upstairs to retrieve our daughter from her room.

They both ran back downstairs, but by this time the fire was so intense it knocked them out, severely burning their bodies.

A neighbor noticed the fire, dashed over, and kicked in the front door. He was able to drag Florence and Jenny out. Our two dogs were barking from their cages that night. They both died from the smoke.

I spent over a year looking for the murderer, with no luck. Then one day, I met a psychologist. In my job as an employee counselor, I was always looking for good therapists to whom I could refer employees. As I got to know him, I found out he was a psychic and a police consultant.

Even though at the time I didn't believe in psychics, I decided to hire him to help me find the murderer. Then, I decided to find another psychic who'd be willing to consult on my case. I chose to employ a well-known psychic. I figured if they both came up with the same person, I would believe it. If they didn't, then it was just a bunch of baloney. I had a reading from each of them.

To my amazement, the psychologist/psychic and the second psychic both came up with the same person! There was just one problem. Since the police had ruined the crime scene, no one would be able to identify any evidence to prove the murderer's identity in court.

The second psychic's name was Linda. When she told me the same thing that the first psychic said, I felt anger rising inside me. I tried to act calm.

"I don't know what I'll do with this information," I said as casually as I could. Linda knew I was lying. I did know what I intended to do. I wanted to kill this person. It was just a matter of figuring out how and when.

Linda could feel the turmoil inside me and spoke calmly. "Bob, your wife and daughter are at peace and don't need you to avenge them. If you do avenge them, it will destroy you."

I paused, reflecting on her well-chosen words. What do I do? I knew her advice was right. Alright, I won't kill the murderer. But what could I do?

"Anyway, your daughter was an old soul who came to teach," said Linda. "Her teaching was finished, and she would have died that year anyway."

I didn't know what she meant at that time and found out later. Through the psychics, I learned the murderer was the ex-wife of the man who my wife was dating! One night, her two daughters even stayed over at our home, playing with my daughter. This infuriated the woman.

She was crazy and jealous. Even though she left her husband, she was upset that he was dating someone else. She wanted to hurt my wife by destroying the house but didn't intend to kill my wife and daughter. Her plan just got out of hand. Obviously, way out of hand.

When I left Linda, I decided not to pursue this crazy woman. I did call the police and told them what I found out. As far as I know, they did nothing with the information.

REFLECTIONS

1. Do you believe in psychics? (I know I didn't up to that time.)
2. Have you ever been in such a desperate situation, and wanted to speak to an outsider who could help?
3. What did you do in your own desperation?
4. How do you handle angry feelings when you want retribution against someone?
5. How are you able to forgive someone who has hurt you or someone you love?

CHAPTER 14
Beginning to Love Myself

How my shoulders and arms kept aching! For over a year, they ached so badly... ever since my time in the hospital with my wife and daughter.

I didn't know what to do.

After I had found out who killed my wife and daughter, I spoke about the pain in my shoulders and arms to a friend of mine. He suggested that I sit down in a rocking chair.

"I want you to start rocking," he said. "Imagine that you're rocking Jenny."

I figured I had nothing to lose, so I did just that. I started rocking and imagined holding Jenny in my arms. Back and forth, back and forth. While I rocked, I started crying. Tears flowed as I kept crying and crying. But as I kept rocking my daughter in my mind, my arms started feeling better. Incredible as it may sound, the pain began going away.

When I was finished rocking Jenny, the pain was gone. Suddenly, I saw myself rocking a little boy. I was shocked and amazed. I realized this little boy was me! Oh, how I hated me. I didn't want anything to do with me. My inner voice was extremely critical of me.

At that moment, I saw that this little boy was no different than my daughter. My beautiful daughter whom I loved with all my heart. How could I be cruel to that little boy when I was so loving to my daughter?

Right then and there, I made a commitment to love myself as I loved my daughter. I needed to learn to talk warmly and lovingly to me. What a revelation! I never thought about how I treated myself before.

Later, I remembered what Linda had said about my daughter being a teacher. I realized that when Jenny was born, she taught me to love. When she died, she left such a big space in my life. I needed to fill that space with love. What Jenny did was teach me to love myself.

Jenny has been my greatest teacher, and I've had some terrific teachers. From Jenny, I discovered my life purpose. It's beyond what I had ever conceived when I first set off on my career. It's a purpose that so many of us need... teaching people to love themselves.

Loving myself was not just making a simple commitment.

I found out there was a lot of work to be done. I became aware of the different beliefs that I acquired as I grew up, and I needed to challenge them to see if they were true. Did those beliefs serve me or not?

Many of my past beliefs I had just accepted because my parents, family, teachers, and others told me they were true.

Some of my past beliefs included:

- There is a hell. If you aren't Catholic, you will go to hell.
- You are a sinner if you are angry, think sexual thoughts, or eat meat on a Friday.
- It's bad if you think about yourself.
- You should always worry about what the neighbors will think.

What I was programmed to believe was you've got to live your life for other people. I never challenged my parents or the church. Inside, I had questions about these beliefs. But I never expressed my doubts. I'd think, "Is this true?" I pushed aside my skepticism. "Must be true," I thought. I even felt bad for questioning what I was told. Then, I created other limiting beliefs from my personal experiences. These examples were:

- I should always please others rather than myself.
- I should always be nice and not get angry.
- I only have value if I am helping others and not for whom I am.

So, what was true?

Looking back to understand myself.

Where do our beliefs start? Look back in the past to the earliest memories. What did we believe as a child? How has that affected us?

My early beliefs are rooted in feeling unworthy. Not good enough. In reflecting on my childhood, I came to believe I wasn't worthwhile when my mother gave me to my grandmother. She literally gave up caring for me and told my grandmother to look after me.

Suddenly, I wasn't really a member of our family! I felt worthless. I was an outsider. To have any value, I believed I needed to do things for others. I wasn't good enough just on my own. Those feelings stayed inside me as I grew up. Feelings get imprinted in our brain, and don't disappear on their own.

My older brother's ongoing fights and shaming me reinforced my feeling of lack. Besides that, I learned to avoid showing my feelings to him, because that would only bring more abuse.

It was the only way to protect myself. Keep those feelings of sadness, anger, resentment inside. No one should know. I didn't even want to know. I didn't want to feel the pain. Year after year, I kept my feelings inside. As the traumas happened - - the losses of my best friend, my cousin and my father, my broken heart couldn't deal with these major upheavals. I learned to shut all my feelings down. It was the only way to cope.

It just hurt too much to feel what I felt. My time in the seminary just added to the belief that it was best not to feel anything. I could manage being numb to the ups and downs around me. But then the fire happened...

With my senses reeling, and discovering the cause behind the fire, I didn't want to face the intense inner pain that was hiding in my heart. My work became an escape.

For a while after the fire, I thought I had made a mistake in doing the body psychotherapy training. I was feeling everything so deeply. TOO deeply!

How could I deal with this onrush of pain?

My mind fought those pent-up feelings that rose like a tidal wave. I've done all this inner work, and what good does it do? I'm just more aware of the pain from my wife's and daughter's loss. How can that help me recover? What good will it do?

There was a lot for me to learn on how to be more loving to myself. I had so many beliefs and habits standing in the way. I was going to experience a lot of mistakes on my journey to self-love. But I was willing to take the first step.

I'm still on that journey. To help you, I'd like to touch on some of the significant parts of my journey that moved me forward.

You never know how one person, one event, or one action can make a difference in your life.

CHAPTER 15
Light at the End of the Tunnel

When you least expect it, sometimes a light appears at the end of a tunnel. That's what happened during the worst point in my life, when I was trying to cope after the house fire turned my life upside down.

At that time, I was working as the Director of Employee Counseling at a pharmaceutical firm and was fortunate to have a graduate student, Bob Wright at my side, handling any emergencies that arose.

We talked about starting our own company. Our aim was to get a contract to counsel the employees at the pharmaceutical company and develop a psychotherapy practice too.

Starting A New Life: Human Effectiveness, Inc.

Everything fell into place, and soon we started Human Effectiveness, Inc. I always said I was too depressed to know better. As it turned out, Bob had studied a form of therapy, an outgrowth from the Adlerian tradition, that focused on helping people challenge their long-held beliefs, so they could create beliefs that worked for them. While I was unfamiliar with this model of therapy, Bob knew its value. He used it for patients individually and in groups.

Before long, Bob got so busy, he reached out to me to lead the Wednesday night group. Do you think I knew what I was doing? Not really...

Although I led groups before, this was different. I didn't know how to lead this type of group! At first, I didn't worry too much about it. Then, when I actually started the group, I hated running it. I didn't know what I was doing.

I felt so inadequate. What were the assignments intended for? Were the group members really doing them correctly? What was I supposed to do?

It wasn't long before I started hating Wednesday nights. Finally, I couldn't take it any longer. I told Bob that he needed to start a training group for me and our other therapists, so we could all learn how to do this type of therapy.

One thing led to another. The training and experience around this therapy challenged many of my own limiting beliefs. It also opened so many doors for me personally. I'll always be grateful to Bob for revealing a new pathway for me to learn and lead.

The Power of Retreats

It's never too late to love oneself, resolve anger and live life with joy.

That's what I discovered when I was led into another path -- leading men's retreats. It started out very innocently. Since my father died before I had a chance to really complete our relationship, I felt a yearning to experience a close friendship with other men. Thinking of the unresolved situations around my father left me with pain.

By divine coincidence (others might reconsider that) I asked Bob to go fishing with me to Canada, a magical place where I loved to fish. Unfortunately, Bob had already booked all his vacation time!

"I'll do it if you can make this part of a business experience," he said. "If I can do it as part of the business, with a higher purpose in mind, I'll go."

"I'm up for the challenge!" I told him. When I get determined, nothing stops me. So, I planned a trip for an adventurous men's retreat in Canada. It included my favorite pastime -- fishing. We enrolled eleven men for a week.

What an exhilarating time we had! We learned a lot too. During this get away from home, we relaxed and came together as a community. We opened up about our lives, our fathers, our issues, and our vision for the future. Little did I know that it would propel me on a journey of healing my relationship with my father, just by helping men work through their father-son relationships.

The positive energy from our time together lasted beyond the week. Several months after that retreat, two of the men approached me. I could tell they had something important on their mind.

"So, Bob, where are we going next year?"

"I'm not planning to go anywhere," I told them. I really wasn't planning on undertaking another retreat for men. The trip was a lot of work -- from start to finish. I figured we made about 25 cents an hour doing the event. Of course, I DID get my opportunity to go fishing.

"What?" they asked me incredulously. "That trip was so great. We learned so much about being men. It was fun, and I know we all grew a lot from the experience. Won't you reconsider?"

Their sincerity stopped me. "You mean -- I can plan to go anywhere I want to go, charge you a reasonable fee for the trip, and you'd want to go?"

"ABSOLUTELY!" they exclaimed.

How could I resist? So, I decided another retreat would be in store for the following year... and the next. We established a track record in our men's work, and we all got to learn so much about ourselves.

Uncovering More Healing Techniques

Once I opened my heart to healing and growth, more opportunities seemed to fall in my lap. As I discovered, we attract what we focus on. My focus became finding solutions in life, not problems. And the universe was responding.

Neuro-Linguistic Programming -- As my healing progressed, I came across a fascinating therapy, Neuro-Linguistic Programming or "NLP." It also added to my inner growth, and

I knew my clients would benefit too. The method impressed me so much that I became a master practitioner in NLP.

Through NLP, I began my journey in understanding how the brain works. I decided to learn how to do hypnosis too. Each of these practices helped me develop my imagination skills, as well as encourage my clients to expand their capabilities too.

Neurofeedback Therapy -- In 1990, I was introduced to neurofeedback by a client. He had been in Florida and had gotten a great deal out of a process called neurofeedback therapy. His enthusiasm impressed me enough to call the neurofeedback practitioner who had worked with him. I asked him if he'd train me and a psychologist that worked for our firm, Human Effectiveness.

"Yes," he replied quickly. "But you've got to be here." The psychologist and I went to Florida for two weeks. For five days each week, we worked with the neurofeedback trainer. The trainer told us what to do. In the morning the psychologist practiced neurofeedback on me, and then I practiced on him. We'd repeat the work in the afternoon. In the two weeks, we each had 20 treatments, and observed the practitioner's treatments on his clients.

Up to that time, whenever I smelled smoke, I would feel upset inside. Ever since the house fire, the smell of smoke was a trigger, releasing an agitation that overwhelmed me. I knew it was an emotional pattern, but I couldn't break out of it. Yet after those two weeks of neurofeedback therapy, the upset didn't happen anymore. It was amazing!

Naturally, I fell in love with neurofeedback from that moment. It's become an indispensable part of my practice, and the equipment keeps getting better and better.

The Deep Breathing Process

Tuning in to the therapy of deep breathing was still another tool that helped me in my growth. Deep breathing has so many benefits, both physically, mentally and spiritually.

I used a coach to help me learn how to properly do deep breathing. It's a process of consciously inhaling and exhaling slowly. Not only did I feel more relaxed, but I experienced a deeper knowledge of myself.

During this therapy, I'd see many images whirling into my mind, moving me to view myself and the world around me differently. I could be apart from my body, centered in a calm state, while an energy of peace and quiet gently flowed through my body. I didn't have to think about anything. Just simply be.

Deep breathing also helped me make peace with God. Before this time, I felt immersed in a big fight with God. I thought God was dyslexic. I thought God must believe my name was Job, not Bob.

"God doesn't love me. That's for sure," I thought. I was tired of fighting with God, and I certainly wasn't winning.

Using the deep breathing process, I decided to get back into a peaceful relationship with God. No more arguments.

In one session, I saw an image of myself wanting to return to God. Walking across a field, I found a person approaching me. To my amazement, I saw that it was none other than God. A radiant, glowing face looked at me tenderly, with the utmost love. Everything in, and around me was love, love, love. Love emanated from this spiritual being, permeating through my whole being.

I couldn't believe it. "God, I thought you didn't love me," I said.

The answer came back loud and clear. "No! I have loved you for all time. I am always here. You just have to want something. You turned that off in you. I don't kick your door down; you have to open it."

I finally understood. My fight with God ended that day, and I've been at peace with God ever since. I realized I had stopped wanting anything from anybody. I had shut down for much of my life. I had learned in my family that wanting only led to disappointment and hurt. As I discovered, wanting something more is essential in our ability to grow as people.

Cognitive Training in Australia

Another big learning experience was right around the corner.

When I visited Australia, I met several cognitive scientists who performed amazing work with children. When I returned to the United States, I called them up to ask them to train me. They said they would not! I didn't give up. I called them every week for two years. Finally, they could tell I wouldn't give up, so they agreed to train me.

I made several trips to Australia for training and invited the scientists over to the United States too. The training helped me deeply appreciate how we learn and grow and how to serve others even better.

Now, I work with children, parents, adults, businesspeople, athletes and even the military. Everyone benefits. Understanding how our wonderful brain works can help us use it so much more effectively.

Insights in Critical Thinking Skills

I especially like to train parents, who can then pass on their wisdom to their children in critical thinking skills. Ultimately, this process allows children to grow naturally and become successful adults. Parenting is an extraordinarily complex skill, and our society does so little to prepare people for parenthood. Parents just get thrown into the water and must learn to swim or drown without much support.

Critical thinking skills is like throwing someone a life preserver. You've got a way to stay afloat.

Here's a fascinating insight about the brain. As part of my training, it became clear that a part of our brain doesn't like anything unfamiliar. This is an early part of the brain, developed to help us survive in a dangerous environment.

When our ancestors lived in trees and were more prey than predators, anything in the environment, that was unfamiliar, could potentially kill them. They avoided anything unknown. The people who didn't have this aspect of their brain highly developed enough became dinner and stopped contributing to the gene pool.

As you can imagine, this part of our brain is highly developed. Our brain broadcasts: *"Stay with familiar circumstances. Avoid anything new, even though it may be good for us. Never leave your comfort zone."* That's the source for most of our procrastination.

How do we get this part of the brain to let go?

Create a truly clear and detailed plan, free of dangers and with plenty of support from others around you.

One thing I teach my clients is how to build that great plan or pathway, then get the necessary support to execute the plan. Once your support plan is in place, procrastination fades away. Results begin to appear. People can now become effective creators in their lives.

Each of our experiences provides a chance for us to learn and grow. I had the privilege and honor of training U.S. Marines in Hawaii, Chicago, and Kansas City, using several areas of Mental Performance Training. I trained the marines in recognizing IED's, improving marksmanship, overall performance, and improved behavior. These brave men and women taught me a great deal too. I hope they learned as much from me as I did from them. I gained an appreciation for the power of making a commitment and respecting both myself and others.

Developing Our Capacity to Love

Through this journey of learning to love myself and others, I've followed several spiritual paths. Each one focused on developing the capacity to love. Expanding our loving capacity helps us grow. So, where does one start?

It all comes down to loving ourselves. Only then can we appreciate and love others more. Sounds simple, right?

Yet, to open ourselves up to love means we need to forgive others and ourselves. This was a hard lesson for me to learn. I felt so righteous about other people being wrong or bad. I'd think about how I had been wronged. I wanted to come up with a plan for striking back. How could I get even?

I realized that by holding onto the pain, I could justify my anger. Inside, I wanted to lash out and hurt others, just as I felt they hurt me. But what was that emotion doing to me? I was causing myself distress. I finally realized the way to freedom was in forgiving them.

Forgiveness isn't just a one-time process. Oh no...

In my anger, I'd often re-indict those who hurt me. Then, I'd have to forgive them again and again. It wasn't always easy.

Now, when I feel anger rising inside, I say a prayer of forgiveness to ask God to help me forgive others, for them to forgive me, and for me to forgive myself. The last part has often been the hardest for me because I'm hard on myself. I learned how to beat myself up a long time ago. And I must admit, I had gotten exceptionally good at beating myself up.

Forgiveness dissolves the negative emotion that weighs us down. When we practice forgiveness, we can love both ourselves and others more deeply. There's a Beatles song, "All we need is love... all we need is love... all we need is love, love... Love is all we need." Isn't that true?

REFLECTIONS

1. Are you still holding onto resentments toward others in your life?
2. If you are, what is that costing you in terms of enjoying your life?
3. What would it take for you to forgive?
4. How much more freedom and joy would you have if you could let go of the pain you hold and forgive?

CHAPTER 16
Your Blank Canvas Is Ready for Creating

Many people feel empty inside. I know I did. Most people think that feeling empty means something is wrong with them. They fret and worry.

"How do I get rid of this emptiness?" they ask me. They look so forlorn. I'd try to fill my own emptiness and that of my clients, but it didn't help.

Here's what I finally realized. The emptiness is supposed to be there. There is *nothing* wrong with someone who feels empty.

When I hear, *"I feel so empty inside!"* my answer is, "Congratulations! That emptiness is your creative workshop. You are a creator and to create means to make something from nothing. This is your nothingness workshop that you create from. It doesn't mean there is no being there. It just means there is an experience of nothing there. It is your blank canvas for creating."

I then ask, "Would you like a tour?" Inevitably, they say, "yes."

I instruct people to close their eyes and find that space of emptiness. "Don't fight the experience or run from it. Just observe the emptiness and notice your experience and breathe."

Before long, clients relax, enjoying that empty space. They realize there is nothing wrong with them. On the contrary, they learn the emptiness is a powerful place to create whatever is on their mind.

It's important to know that what we imagine and visualize tends to show up in our lives. It's like ordering from the menu of the universe. Be specific about what you want. Order with a positive intention.

If you're feeling negative about yourself and the world, that's what you are most likely going to receive. I urge you to carefully think through what you want. Since you get to choose what you want, focus on a positive outcome.

Use your imagination to attract what you want to receive in the world. Your mind can help you find your ideal job, the perfect partner in life, or the wonderful place where you want to live.

Take the time to write down your vision. It has been proven that those who write down their goals have a higher chance of achieving them.

Remember: miracles can happen. You just have to be open to believing.

REFLECTIONS

1. How much do you believe in the power of your imagination?

2. How much do you use your imagination in your daily life to create what you want?

3. How much were you encouraged to use your imagination in your family?

4. Did you know nothing was created in this world without imagination coming first?

CHAPTER 17
Exercises in Loving Yourself

When I imagined rocking my daughter, trying to stop my arms from aching, I ended up rocking myself as a little boy. By learning to love my child inside, I learned how to be more loving to my adult self.

Exercise #1: Loving Your Inner Child.

Close your eyes and begin to breathe deeply. Now imagine your little child inside and quietly to yourself say hi to him/her. Whatever age your child shows up as is fine.

Now imagine putting your child on your lap and putting your arms around him/her. I want you to look into your child's eyes and quietly to yourself say that you want to apologize to him/her for having to leave him/her so long ago. Tell him/her that you didn't know what else to do because you didn't know how to take care of him/her then. Tell your child you are back now and never want to leave him/her again and you want to learn how to take good care of him/her.

Tell your child that you need him/her in your life as he/she is the source of your feelings and creativity and your connection to the universe.

Now, put one of your hands over your child's heart and imagine white light coming out of the palm of your hand and your fingertips. Imagine this white light penetrates his/her chest and enters your child's heart. This white light is a healing and loving light. It enters your child's heart and fills it with love and healing. Watch how the white begins to heal the wounds that your child has. Imagine how the light grows with each of your breaths and begins to fill up your child's body and that of you, the big person.

Tell the child that you want to have some tangible symbol that will represent the child inside so that you don't forget him/her. It can be an object, picture, doll, stuffed animal or anything else. The two of you should agree on it and it then can remind you to always think of your child.

Spend some time getting to know your child and how you best can take care of him/her. Find out how he/she feels and what it has been like to be with your child. Tell him /her that you want to be in constant touch so you can work together. Now come on back to the room and let's talk about your experience.

I know you may think this is weird or crazy, but we have many facets to ourselves, much like a diamond. There is a childlike energy in all of us, and we need to tap into it and nurture it. This is just one way to do it.

I have done this with hundreds of people and each person has their own unique experience. I find it begins to make a big difference in how they experience life.

Most panic attacks and anxiety results from the inner child not feeling heard or tended to. The only power it has is to let the big part of us know that he/she is not happy by giving us a panic attack or lots of anxiety. When the client really starts relating well to the child inside, the panic and anxiety go away.

Exercise #2: Checking in With Your Inner Child.

To stay in touch with my inner child, I've used several techniques. You can follow the same guidelines. Look in a mirror and greet yourself with love. Here's what I do...

Gazing at the mirror, I look in my eyes, searching for my little boy. I then say, "Hi, Bobby! It is great to see you today! I hope we have a good time together!"

Another thing to do is to ask three questions. I rate my answers on a 0 to 10 scale. The first is, "How alive am I feeling?" The second is, "How much am I playing?" The third is, "Does my play have direction?"

These questions keep me in touch with my inner child and on "purpose". They can do the same for you! Your inner child will appreciate your kindness.

REFLECTIONS

1. How in touch are you with your inner child?
2. What can you do to nurture your inner child?
3. How well do you treat your inner child?
4. By being in a good relationship with your inner child, you become more creative and experience greater joy.
5. When you speak to your inner child, what do you hear?
6. What creativity do you feel needs to be expressed?

Exercise #3:   Make Your Inner Critic Your Ally.

Most of us have inner critics. They are often not very nice. They put us down, call us names and regularly shame us. They were developed to protect us as we grew up. They are trying to criticize us before others have a chance to criticize us.

Those of us who have these critics, were often raised in critical homes or homes where we got no feedback. Our critics are trying to be helpful, but in actuality, they cause us a good deal of trouble and undermine our confidence. The inner critic can keep us from engaging successfully in the world.

I recommend having a meaningful conversation with your critic.

Here's what you can say, "Thank you critic, for your efforts to protect me. But I need you to take on a different job. The job I suggest is to be my bodyguard. Guard me against harsh criticism from the outside world. Would you be willing to do that?"

It may take a few conversations but keep at it. You can make your critic your ally rather than your adversary. And it will make your life more enjoyable and fulfilling.

Remember -- YOU are in charge. So, choose how you want to live.

REFLECTIONS

1. Are you aware of an inner critic that you have?

2. How does your critic talk to you?

3. What effect does your critic have on you?

4. Could you imagine how you could be more supportive of yourself?

CONCLUSION

My hope is this book has been of service to you.

I still see clients, as I enjoy each day and learn so much. I hope that you can use what you've read, so you can love yourselves and others more.

The more love you bring to the world, the better this world becomes. Each of us makes a difference.

Please help raise the positive vibration of our planet so we all can benefit.

At Critical Thinking for Success LLC, we're dedicated to learning more, so we can serve our clients more fully. Each person is treated with respect and love.

If you are interested in what we are doing, please reach out and contact us. look forward to talking with you.

Visit: www.Criticalthinkingforsuccess.com

About the Author

Robert Kauffman, Founder of Critical Thinking for Success, LLC is a popular neurofeedback therapist, brain expert, and psychotherapist whose expertise has transformed the lives of youth, adults and seniors alike.

Through in-depth training and therapies, Robert helps companies increase revenues and profits, decrease costs, improve leadership, reduce stress, become more innovative, and have fun.

In helping the brain balance itself, Robert's clients think more efficiently, sleep better and stay focused longer. This has been especially useful for those with ADD/ADHD, head injuries such as concussions, PTSD, learning problems, headaches, depression, anxiety, and panic attacks.

Robert's ability to provide love, compassion and understanding comes from having overcome enormous trauma, grief and upheaval in his own life. Robert's story is like none other – a testimony to the courage of the human spirit -- and how guidance from the Other Side can help each of us in learning to love oneself.

Through this memoir, Robert's story brings readers profound, spiritual insights about life, love and forgiveness. His lessons ultimately apply to each of us.

We all are on Earth school to learn about loving oneself. Give yourself permission to apply his tips to your own life. This book can change the way you look at your life forever.